scab.

I0560242

scab.

annamarie d.

THE
GRIT & GRACE
PRESS

for the ones that mistook me for weak.
may every time you hear my name
taste like blood in your mouth.

*and lo, she rose not from grace, but from grit-with
dirt on her knees and fire on her tongue*

i didn't write these to make peace.
i wrote them to bleed without apologizing.
this book isn't polished. it's not soft.
this book is not about healing. it's about what comes before.
it's the sting, the mess, the skin you peel back when it itches too long.
scab is every time i bit my tongue and tasted iron.
it's every red flag i turned into a ribbon.
it's every time i stayed quiet and hated myself for it.
scab is what happens when you finally stop pretending it didn't hurt.
some of these poems are prayers, some are curses.
these words are not neat. they are not healed.
but they're real. and they're mine.

-annamarie d.

i love the way you grip my skin
holding on tight
making sure the only place i slip is into oblivion

wrap your arms around me baby
let's take this ride together
hold on tight don't let go

i hold a grudge the same way i held my mothers
hand crossing a busy street
careful not to let go
scared of what might happen if i do

how many times will it take for me to realize that
this version of a man is just a reflection of me
i'm not attracted to them, i'm attracted to me
i don't love them, i love me
when i finally realize this i'll find a man that is
actually worth my time and energy

you used to be a statue in the garden of my mind
the flowers flourished around you and accentuated
your beauty
but soon the clouds turned gray
and as the water beat down on your stone
you slowly started to crumble
and once the clouds have gone
and the sun has returned
the flowers flourished
and you were gone

i've always been a take what you need kind of
person
with my poetry
my love
my body
my brain

when you tell me you love me it's just syllables
strung together
your actions do not match the noises coming from
your mouth
"i love you"
when? can you explain to me in excruciating detail
how to even love me?
because this is not it
this is much more like hate

go ahead and steal my thunder
remember i'm the lightning
i'm the whole damn storm

once the pen hits the paper
you will live forever
you will forever be the person i mold you into
the words i string together create the man i
thought you were

our love comes in waves
it does not ebb and flow
it is not like ocean waves
the more intense
the higher the length
our love lives in the laughter
the chatter
the sighs
the tears

you taste so good on my lips

staring at the ocean i imagined what it would be
like to float amongst the waves
the same way, as a child, i would stare up at the
sky and imagine what it would be like to float on a
cloud
to be weightless and carefree
maybe it's just my childhood i'm missing

baby flow to me
let the water fill the gaps
engulf me
swallow me whole

i have always had an obsession with worship
praying to my anxieties everyday
devoting myself to the pain
begging on my knees for the pleasure
sacrificing my body to you everyday

i like my coffee when i chase it down with you

your words wrap around me like silk

it's like i found a secret garden
when i moseyed around
there was one secret revealed to me
and that secret was me
all along i just needed to find myself
be myself
and the world would be mine
anything i could've ever dreamed
belongs to me

were you only attracted to the idea of me?
the lore i give off
the person you perceived me as
i think that's it
you thought i was someone i wasn't
and when i refused to shove myself into your
container
you went and found someone who willingly
shrunk themselves to fit
so you say i was the bullet you dodged
but ill always be the one you think about
the one that caused you to question yourself
to make you wonder why you're not enough
i could be the reason you change
or the reason you end up resenting
i'll just stay as a reflection of you

do you know what it's like to lose control
to be so powerless to another soul

i keep holding onto to the person you were
and that keeps holding me back
my past is like an anchor holding me down
and now i'm stuck in the open water alone

your slang has changed and it sounds awfully
familiar
you're not the person you were
you've consumed too much and now you're lost
tell me when you look in the mirror, who do you
see?
is it me?
i know i sparked something in you
i will always be the sun casting light on your world
get comfortable in my shadow
because that's where you'll always be

i love when you pick my petals one by one

savoring each moment
opening me up just for you
revealing every part of me
embrace the beauty
embrace me

i think i am a placeholder
i am someone who holds the space for everyone
else
i will hold you up and guide you to where you need
to be
i will get you ready and build your confidence
once you are gone i am still in the same place
i have not even taken half a step forward
i fall behind
not one person stops to grab my hand or even ask
if i need help
i tell you i am struggling and you still step on my
shoulders to get ahead
i can scream for help until there's no more air in
my lungs
but it is like i am a ghost
i float through life
never being seen
never being heard
i will reach for help at every corner and still fall
short
i try so hard but it is like i am running in place
i worry my legs may get tired and i will have
nobody to carry me to the end of this race
what if i am not strong enough
will my love carry me through, like it does for
everyone else?

you handed me insecurities like a family heirloom
constantly holding my head under the water
barely letting me come up for air
i understand you chose to live your life a certain
way
but i refuse to do that
i refuse to settle
i will get everything i want out of this life
i will take and take and take
until i reach every goal and every dream
i am steering this ship and i will not let you
capsize it

i watch the negative thoughts pile up like the dirty
plates in the sink
i tell myself one more nap and then i'll put the
laundry away
just five more minutes of scrolling
and then i'll finally get something done
but then the sun goes down so i think i'll get some
rest
i'll be better when i wake
the alarm blares in my face
and i'll hit snooze until the last possible second
then i'll drag myself from bed
great another day
i can tell myself today will be different
but i know it'll be the same
maybe one little change will help me escape

your lips tasted like war
every kiss rained fire on my mind
every touch like a bomb going off throughout my
body
my mind plays a symphony of chaos
we indulge in the battle any chance we get
i take blow after blow
and still stand at your front line
a woman of your valor

baby we are just too stars colliding
we knew this would explode
but it feels so damn good

i am the altar baby
kneel before me
show me your offering
drive me crazy
be my sacrifice

lift my chin
i want to make eye contact with my sin
watch me take all of this in
study every inch of my body
a sacred relic
kneeling upon a desecrated shrine
let me worship you
welcome to the pearly gates

you think you can pull the rug from under my feet
but did you forget you are the one that
taught me how to hold it down

i just love being alone so much
it gives me butterflies to think about how i can
control my own life
and when i'm alone i have complete control
what was done to me to make me cherish
solitude so much

i long for restraint
to be held back
to beg for more

sometimes i wish i could go back to the start
when our laughter was loud and wild
our hearts were full
and fun was had
back to where the hurt did not reside
before my heart shattered into a million pieces
before you placed your dark clouds in my baby
blue sky
is it possible to get back to that place

i rearrange my life to find the perfect place for you
i declutter my mind so you have a place to live
but fitting you into my life was not what you
wanted
you were just passing through
you had no intentions of settling in

once i took my glasses off it was like i was able to
see clearly
i do not recognize you
the man i knew never would have used that
language with me
you have turned into someone i despise
you are a stranger now

i would tear down this whole world to get your
attention
wreak havoc to everything around you
just to get one glance from you

you lit a fire in me
now i can't stop dancing around the flames
you are lighting up the center of my universe
the heat moves through my body
i burn my fingers trying to touch you
i would let you burn my whole world down

how could a few shapes and syllables carry so
much weight
tie them together to make something so beautiful
it will bring tears to your eyes
tie them together to make something so terrible
your soul completely shatters
these shapes and syllables carry more power than
the sun
yet get thrown around like garbage

i want to dance with you the way the sun dances
with the water on a hot summer day
i want to grow with you the way daffodils bloom
on a warm spring afternoon
i want to fall for you so completely and
shamelessly like the leaves do on a crisp autumn
morning
i want to kiss you the way each glistening
snowflake slowly kisses the earth on a cold
winter's evening
i want you for every season

i don't wake up and search for your name in my
notifications anymore
i sleep better at night not waiting for your
response
you put yourself on do not disturb
soon the line will be dead

i wonder what winter you froze in
what happened to you
now your stuck in an endless loop of darkness and
ice
maybe you loved me because i am summer
you thought my sunshine would melt your icy
heart
and brighten your universe
but your darkness dulled my shine
it was not long before my summer turned into fall
all my seasons blended together into one long
frigid winter
you were gone
searching for sunshine
while i was stuck in the cold

you only starve me when you know i'm craving you

the conditions for loving me are not on your terms
you do not make the rules for how to handle me
this is my life
you are not the center of my universe

you like to keep me in the dark
hidden from the world
hidden from the truth
in the shadows you can not see the bruises
time dulls the scars
darkness engulfs me
always a part of me

i bought the old cleaning spray you liked
i haven't used it in forever
the moment the spray left the bottle i was taken
back to that night
a night of sneaking around
drinking wine
talking
laughing

i knew that night that i would be carving my own
cross
and still i took a step in your direction
one more sip
one more kiss
and the music is still playing
on repeat

the anger inside him raged like a caged beast
every sip just added fuel to the fire
every step the beast roared more and more
finally finding release
at the expense of my skin
of my body
of my mind

i woke up that morning in a haze
i walk through the cloud of smoke
i thought you would be there when it cleared
i rack my brain trying to remember the last time i
felt you
your memory slips my mind
it fades to pieces of dust
that sit in that old house
with the memories and the love

i hope in another life you make time for me
i hope in another life you call me back
i hope in another life i get all of you
not just the breadcrumbs you leave behind

our love was a house of cards
one false move and we'll collapse

as i consult an empty glass
i can't help but ask
was it my fault?
i really *really* didn't need that last drink
and i really didn't need to say those words you
insist i did
funny because i don't remember a thing
i ask the glass once more
was it my fault?
no it was yours

i carve my name in the walls of your heart
flowing through your veins
i am the air you breathe
once you have a piece of me you'll never be the
same

it is not fair that you get to go on and live your life
while i am stuck trying to clean up the pieces of
mine
but that's how it always was wasn't it?
you run through the house like bat out of hell
just for me to clean up the mess you made

i pray one day i could love someone without eating
them alive

what would it take for you to miss me
for you to want me
would i have to completely erase myself from your
life
act like you never existed
would that bring you back to me

i was a ripe fruit dangling from a tree
dripping with lechery
of course you would want to take a bite out of me

i spent the morning slowly drinking my coffee
outside
alone with myself and my thoughts
the birds chirping
cicadas singing
being one with earth
with life
this is contentment
this is what life is about

i put my heart on a platter for you
you cut into it like a rare steak
savoring each bite
slowly killing me
with the blood dripping from your mouth
i couldn't love you more

i howl for you like a wolf howls at the moon

there is a universe where i slipped my hand in yours
when you walked me to class instead of taking a step
away
there is a universe where i let you know how grateful i
was for the coffee you would bring me
there is a universe where i smiled at you as you watched
me study
there is a universe where i actually went on the date you
wrote in my planner
there is a universe where i told you how much i thought
about your smile as i stared at you across the table,
while you jokingly picked on me
there is a universe where we are singing along to zac
brown band with your arms around my shoulders
there is a universe where i am part of the happy life you
created
but we're in this universe
i could only hope that in another universe we are *knee
deep in the water somewhere*

i can not tell you what i was wearing the night we
met
i do not remember the first time you were
introduced to me
i do remember the respect you showed me
i remember how much you cared
your half smile and sparkle in your eye is
imprinted on my brain
i yearn for that smile like the starless sky craves
the moon light
i will patiently wait for the day your eyes lay upon
me again

i stood at the fork in the road
weighing my options
both paths appealing in their own way
i chose the path with the pretty flowers
i saw the thorns
told myself i just wouldn't touch them
the further i moved down the path
the flowers started to wilt
the storm clouds formed
the rain came down fast and hard
yet the flowers never started to grow again
the soil was rotted
it was too late to turn around

maybe i like flowers so much because im
mourning the woman i was yesterday

you handed me a winter coat when the ice started
to form
i said no
you insisted i needed a coat, that i would freeze
and i insisted i did not need it
i froze
the frostbite started in my hands
i couldn't feel
it crept down to my feet
i couldn't run
i reached for that coat when my heart started to
freeze
i should have listened

i wish my red lipstick was lovingly kissed off of my
face
rather than violently wiped away

will you still want to kiss my lips
even though they taste bitter from others before
will you still want to hold my hands when theyre
frozen from the past
will you still walk with me even if i have cold feet

so many lives being lived at one time
it would be easy for them to blur together
but there are walls and insulation blocking
us from each other
setting a firm border between our universes

you showed me off like a prized pig
and here's a little secret, i loved it
feeling everyone's eyes on me
knowing i'm the object of their desire
lighting the fire inside of them
it's the fuel that keeps me going

lately i have been falling asleep next to a ghost
i cuddle up to him and hold him tight
and every night he tells me stories of lives once
lived
he rubs my back
kisses my forehead
comforts me until i fade into sleep
i wake up cold and alone and wonder where he
went
he is only here at night
i only get him in a glimmer under the sun

your hands were like a record player
every touch played a song
making my body move to the rhythm
every breath set the pace
my body naturally danced to your song

my favorite shade of pink is the color of my lips
when you leave

the subtle hip grab when were walking through a
crowd
the gaze across the room
the whispers nobody hears
a budding romance

you always picked me because im ripe
like a secret on the verge of spilling heavy with the
weight of truth
you want me to take the first bite
you want to see the juice spilling from my lips
you watch me lick my lips clean
ready to take a piece of me

you do not put me together
you do not hold on so tight that i can not move
you open me up
you let me breathe
you let me take up space
you let me be me
let me be raw

my brain burns with guilt
while my skin shivers with your touch
and my body softens in your presence
how easy it is to get lost in the midst of sin

can i dream about you one last time
before i let you go
conjure up every scenario that would make you
perfect
but only in my head
romanticize the miniscule things you did
and then turn them into standards to be allowed in
my life
all must abide by the great king that once ruled
the king that made no effort yet got all the praise

your hand traced its way down my back
settling at the base of my hips
lips linked together like an unbreakable chain
every touch brings me closer to god

we live in the shadows
those quiet echoes of laughter
like a ghost of a child running down the hall
only our eyes have adjusted to the darkness
nobody else can see our intense stares
only in the shadows do we get to explore our
bodies
the shadows become the playground of two lovers
who can not speak
only in the shadows is our secret free

you were born under the pale moonlight
after a few drinks and a few lusty kisses
nurtured in parking lots and whispers
what an entanglement we have weaved
you tied us together like sheet bend knot

there is a grey ball of energy sitting in my chest
torn between loving the life i have
and wondering what if

when the stars are filling the sky
and the moonlight is kissing the window pane
i cling tight to the ghosts
in our sweet caress i whisper stories
i fill the air with tales about you

when you look at me with those brown eyes
clutching to me like molasses
you slowly immerse me in you
dripping around me like sweetest shadows
every drop holds the density of our lust

the new lines on my face
the change in my body
it's all proof that time goes by
and i always make it through

i hold on to my trauma like a newborn baby
"don't you dare talk about it like that"
"you don't know it as well as i do"
i cradle it as it grows and grows
eventually the weight is too heavy to carry
i could've stopped coddling it
i could've shared to weight
i could've become stronger so it wouldn't feel so
heavy
i could've asked for help

i will not be judged based on the love that was
given to me
it does not define me
my love is what defines me
so when you take the time to weed through the
forests of my mind
know there will always be sunshine

the dance of toxicity always starts so smooth
gliding and intertwining bodies
movements that could make one jealous
once the spotlight moves away is when the glass
begins to break
falling to the floor creating obstacles for our once
smooth movements
now each move is calculated
each move is well thought out before each step
each step is in the opposite direction
and once our feet are cut up and torn
there is no going back

i want you down to my bones
i need to feel your teeth breaking the skin
your grip on my reality
your body in my dreams
your breath in my mouth
i want to be consumed

one glance in my direction
i am stripped down to my bones
i shed my skin for you
i bare it all
feel me down to my core
lick my soul

i clench my fist at the thought of you
standing white knuckled in front of you
throwing swings any chance i get
blow
by
blow
the tears fall
and all i wanted was for you to hold my hand

dive into me
swim in my depths
once you get too deep there is no way out

i swallowed down the pain as if it was honey
i licked my lips and begged for more
somewhere along the lines
i confused pain with comfort
the ups and downs started to feel like home

the problem is there are so many lives being lived
inside this tiny rectangle in my hands
sending little hits of dopamine to my brain
no wonder we all feel a little mad

just another trophy on your shelf
shiny and new
still making you proud when you walk past
time passes and dust gathers
until the old tarnished trophy turns into
another knick knack you will just stash away

there is something about october that makes me
want to burn everything to the ground
it is the season of death
and i am dying to celebrate
i want to watch everything turn to ash
i want to walk into my new life with the warmth of
my burning past on my skin

you think you are god in my eyes
you have visions of prophecies
of me worshipping even the smallest thought of
you
you think i pray on my knees for you every night
baby you are just a passerby
a jester for my own personal entertainment
i am willing to let this die

how do i write about someone i don't even know
anymore
how can i feel the longing to be your friend again
feel the pain of losing you
when it has been a decade since i have seen you
i mourn the girl i knew
my friend

you walk around in what you call masculinity
it is just a shield to cover all your insecurities
it is like you know deep down that you are pitiful
and a sorry excuse of a man
instead of changing into what you want to be
you seek validation from the men in your life
not even realizing you will never be like them
you will always be covered in shame
grow up

you walk away and i feel the bridge slowly start to
catch fire
the warmth on my skin
the smoke in my nose
i start to flirt with the flames
you waltz right back in time to put the fire out
each time you walk away don't you see the bridge
slowly deteriorate
will you swim to me when there is nothing left
only to find that i no longer wait

i no longer want to shine my spotlight on you
my bulb burns bright but your theatrics are
burning me out
it's not that i can't keep up it's that i don't want to
i no longer want to entertain your games

you pushed me into his arms
you forced me onto his lap
you left a bitter taste
that made his tongue taste like sweetness in my
mouth
you were too busy in your own world to see my lips
stained
and swollen from the bite of another

you forgot who i am
you painted this picture of a lost puppy in your
head
the girl who would follow you around and you
were the only one who could save me
take a step back
i am not a puppy
you will hear my growl

i am a lioness who thoroughly stalked her prey
and like the queen of the jungle i like to play with
my food before i eat it
you may enjoy the chase but i carved the path your
running down
it was all just a game

you are so easily falling into the intricate web i
weaved
just for you
each step you get more stuck
play all you want but im always two steps ahead
i will always come before you

the promise of pleasure was a honey trap
sweet
sticky
no escape

every time i look in the windows of my heart
they are fogged up with remnants of you
the condensation slowly dripping
a reminder of your slow touches on my skin
you know every crack in my foundation
you carefully step not to make a noise

this is a collection of love letters to you
one day you'll open your eyes

i always wanted to go back to the before
but the before put me in this position
the before opened up this door for me
i need to be in the after
in the position to close doors

how many times can you walk through my door
tail between your legs
ready to spread mine
and sweep my feelings under rug
only to walk all over me
and do the same thing over
and over
and over
wiping your feet on the door mat that you made
me
only a matter of time until i am clean

mr big shot you think the spot lights on you
you speak your mind and tell your jokes
the laughter doesn't mean anything
it's just to appease
you only see you
nobody thinks twice
except me

i'm torn between wanting to see you and telling
you to go fuck yourself
i don't want to be split in half anymore
in a constant state of confusion
walking in circles trying to find a reason
waiting for you to make the time
holding on to something i don't even know is real

we tempt each other to say it
throwing stones
waiting
it's done
but neither of us say those words
each stone bigger
how long until the surface cracks

you flew around my hive finding a way in
trying to be a good boy for the queen
you put in the work
what you didn't know
was the pleasure was a trap

you need to pay for your actions
and the price is much higher than you ever would
of thought
it is your life
you gave me the opportunity to ruin it
and guess what baby, i'm doing it
you have begged me and begged me over and over
for this
so don't act surprised when this blows up in your
face

you lock me in a prison of uncertainty

i fed your ego
made it nice and meaty
now when i take a bite out of it
the blood is sweet

you thought you cut out my tongue with your
tender touches and acts of love
my nails are wrapped around your heart
and i'm hungry for blood
one one squeeze and i'm satiated

every time my heart breaks
i hate the pain
it's so uncomfortable
it's only through this pain i find art
i find release
i find love

you baptized me in your blood
baby you gave me enough power to become jesus
and enough hatred to reign punishment on
judgment day
send your complaints to another god
because i am not in the game of sympathy

you are a fogging mirror
each day it is getting harder
and harder to see you
for you who you really are

my hands burn with stories of you
the bumps and ridges
every imperfection
with a mind of their own they move

just like the leaves have had their moment
so did we
so let's unpack our winter coats
and move on from this season

some days it is like the veil has been lifted
and my skin is as a raw as an open wound
a simple touch would set me on fire
a kiss would cause me to combust

who will i be when my eyes will no longer search
for you
and my brain no longer creates stories of you

i lower my face to you
as your scent kisses my senses
i want to bottle this up
save it for those dark rainy days

somewhere along the lines dancing and clubs
 have turned into coffee shops and deep
conversations
smoke breaks have turned into five minute phone
calls
driving around aimlessly has turned into cozy
nights in
conversations dripping with gossip has turned
into conversations about life
growing up has become such a beautiful transition
in this life

i always think that maybe i fell from grace
i was never supposed to be this way
but then when i back up and take a look
maybe this is who i was from the start

every touch sent electricity through my veins
setting me on fire
a smoke signal of desire
calling out for you

illicitly braiding sweet nothings
into the same story we have been spoon fed since
we were young
this is the way it was meant to be
our story was written out before we even began
there is no undoing
no changing

your teeth are begging for my flesh
tongue lapping for my blood

i have been hiding lovers in books
words
sentences
syllables

this is not a passage in time
you are the blood in my veins
filling my life with the sweetest crimson

our secrets live in the safety of the backseat

i think i get a lot of tough love because im too soft
i let too much go
like the saying if you dont stand for anything you
will fall for anything

i am trying to find the cracks in your exterior
to let my light in
you are so damn good at hiding them
i swing my bloody sword
in attempt to create enough openings to let my
light in

find religion in the unholy

cross your heart
hope to die
play this game
and soon the sight of me
will be like needles in your eyes

your hands are calloused from fisting your anger
it doesn't have to be this rough
learn to let go
be free

you had your own idea in your head
you did not even see the classic magic trick
look at my left hand while i caress someone new
with my right

your teeth want to bite into my flesh
eyes following the stream of sweat
my skin is well aware it is being stalked
blistering up with hope

every time you hurt me
it is like you shed a layer of skin
layer after layer
until you're just a skeleton
a reminder of what has been

such sweet venom flowing from your brain to your
lips
slicing holes right into my heart
releasing the crimson river of all the love i had to
give
leaving me empty
in a pool of what ifs

annamarie d. writes like a bruise in bloom. her words are tender, aching, and unapologetically raw. she traces the soft curves of sin and survival, stitching together heartbreak, lust, and longing with a reverent hand. "scab.", her second collection, explores what is buried beneath beauty and ruin. when she is not writing, she's on the mats breaking grips at jiu jitsu or mothering with fierce grace. she is proof that a woman can be both the sanctuary and the storm.

find her on instagram: @annamaried_poetry

scab. is a collection for the ones who bled quietly.

in this follow-up to her debut raw. annamarie d. delivers a body of work that doesn't shy away from the bruised, blistered and barely healing parts of being human. especially as a woman.

these poems hold hands with pain. they confess. they worship.

www.ingramcontent.com/pod-product-compliance
Lightning Source LLC
Chambersburg PA
CBHW070334130626

46556CB00007B/2861